Masters of Music

THE WORLD'S GREATEST COMPOSERS

The Life and Times of

Johann Sebastian Bach

Mitchell Lane
PUBLISHERS

P.O. Box 196
Hockessin, Delaware 19707

Masters of Music
THE WORLD'S GREATEST COMPOSERS

Titles in the Series

The Life and Times of...

Visit us on the web: www.mitchelllane.com
Comments? email us: mitchelllane@mitchelllane.com

Masters of Music
THE WORLD'S GREATEST COMPOSERS

The Life and Times of

Johann Sebastian Bach

by Jim Whiting

Copyright © 2004 by Mitchell Lane Publishers, Inc. All rights reserved. No part of this book may be reproduced without written permission from the publisher. Printed and bound in the United States of America.

Printing   1   2   3   4   5   6   7   8

Library of Congress Cataloging-in-Publication Data
Whiting, Jim, 1943-
    Johann Sebastian Bach/Jim Whiting.
         p. cm. — (Masters of music: World's greatest composers)
    Summary: Discusses the life and career of the eighteenth-century German composer and organist.
    Includes bibliographical references (p.) and index.
        ISBN 1-58415-191-9 (lib bdg.)
    1. Bach, Johann Sebastian, 1685-1750—Juvenile literature. 2. Composers—Germany—Biography—Juvenile literature. [1. Bach, Johann Sebastian, 1685-1750. 2. Composers.] I. Title. II. Series.
    ML3930.B2 W57 2003
    780' .92—dc21
                                        2002153210

ABOUT THE AUTHOR: Jim Whiting has been a journalist, writer, editor, and photographer for more than 20 years. In addition to a lengthy stint as publisher of *Northwest Runner* magazine, Mr. Whiting has contributed articles to the *Seattle Times*, *Conde Nast Traveler*, *Newsday*, and *Saturday Evening Post*. He has edited more than 60 titles in the Mitchell Lane Real-Life Reader Biography series, Unlocking the Secrets of Science and other series. He is the author of numerous books for young adults, including *Juan Ponce de Leon, Francisco Vasquez de Coronado, Charles Schulz,* and *Otto Hahn and the Story of Nuclear Fission*. He lives in Washington state with his wife and two teenage sons.

PHOTO CREDITS: Cover: SuperStock; p. 6 Photo Researchers; p.9 AP Photo/John Rottet; p. 10 Photo Researchers; p. 12 SuperStock/ET Archive, London; p. 15 Wolfgang Kaehler/Corbis; p. 17 Archivo Iconografico, SA/Corbis; p. 20 Hulton/Archive; p. 22 Archivo Iconografico, SA/Corbis; p. 24 Bettmann/Corbis; pp. 26, 32, 33 Photo Researchers; p. 34 Hulton/Archive; p. 36 Bettmann/Corbis; p. 38 Photo Researchers; p. 41 Corbis; p. 42 (left and right) Richard Klune/Corbis.

PUBLISHER'S NOTE: This story is based on the author's extensive research, which he believes to be accurate. Documentation of such research is contained on page 46.

The internet sites referenced herein were active as of the publication date. Due to the fleeting nature of some Web sites, we cannot guarantee they will all be active when you are reading this book.

Contents

The Life and Times of
Johann Sebastian Bach

by Jim Whiting

* For Your Information

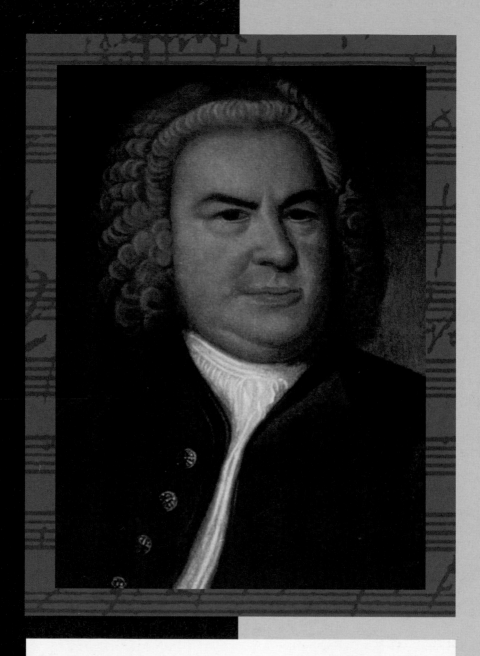

Very few portraits of Bach have been passed down through time. Those that have survived, all with Bach wearing a wig, which was the custom of the day, show many points in common. There are the prominent nose, the fleshy cheeks, the outthrust chin, and a strong, masculine face. A survey of his skeleton in 1894 has indicated that he was about 5 feet, 7 1/2 inches tall. This portrait is from the one done by Elias Gottlieb Haussmann submitted in 1747 to L. C. Mizler's Society of Musical Sciences.

Masters of Music

CHAPTER I

A Towering Reputation

Almost every famous musical composer is easily identifiable by his last name. When we mention Beethoven, we're talking about Ludwig. He wrote the famous Fifth Symphony with its *duh-duh-duh*-*DUH* opening.

Tchaikovsky can only mean Peter, who composed *The Nutcracker.* This ballet is a beloved part of the Christmas season.

Mozart is Wolfgang Amadeus, who wrote 41 symphonies, 27 piano concertos, 20 operas and hundreds of other compositions during his lifetime of just thirty-five years.

But according to *Grove's Dictionary of Music and Musicians,* there are at least 38 composers with the last name of Bach. Another source puts the number at 53. A third says nearly 80. Yet when we refer to "Bach," almost always we mean Johann Sebastian. He is generally regarded as one of the world's three greatest composers, along with Beethoven and Mozart. The standard catalog of his works lists 1,087 different pieces of music.

It can be argued that no one has composed better music for the majestic pipe organ. Every year, hundreds of thousands of people pack music halls to listen to the world's greatest organists play music that Bach wrote more than 250 years ago.

He also wrote some of the greatest music for the human voice. He was the supreme composer of what is called Baroque music. Baroque is characterized by several melodic lines, contrasts between solo and choral voices, drama, and a great deal of ornamentation.

What makes his reputation even more impressive is that for nearly eighty years after his death in 1750, his music was almost entirely ignored. At the end of his life, people believed that he was out of date. His sons, many people said, were composing better and more interesting music. Their father's style was no longer popular.

Yet many popular musicians in recent years have given credit to Bach. The Beatles used the trumpet solo from one of Bach's *Brandenburg Concertos* in one of their most famous songs, "Penny Lane." Some of Bach's compositions are played on electric guitars and sound as if they could have been written today.

He is especially popular among jazz musicians, who often take a simple theme and then improvise variations on it. Fats Waller, a famous jazz pianist, composer and singer of the 1930s and 1940s, greatly admired Bach. Studs Terkel wrote about Waller in his book *Giants of Jazz*: "Next to Lincoln, Johann Sebastian Bach was his number-one hero. He was up till all hours . . . playing Bach on the organ just for himself, for nobody else. A behemoth of a man, all alone in the house, playing, listening, marveling at the genius of the great German."

Bach's music is also used in movie sound tracks and advertising jingles. Films such as *Fantasia, Rollerball, 20,000 Leagues Under the Sea* and *Phantom of the Opera* include his Toccata and Fugue in D Minor.

The Paul Taylor Dance Company rehearses in Page Auditorium at Duke University on July 22, 1999. The lyrical composition they are dancing to is set to movements from Johann Sebastian Bach's fourth, fifth, and seventh concertos for piano and orchestra.

And his Air on a G String can be heard in several movies, including the James Bond film *The Spy Who Loved Me.* The same tune is also used in England in cigar advertisements.

His influence has even spread beyond music. In 2001, Taiwanese painter Paul Chiang had an exhibition that included a series of twenty-four huge paintings called *Meditations on Eternity.* In an interview during the opening, Chiang said that among classical composers, "Bach is the closest to oriental thought. He conveys something close to eternity. I always played his music while working on this series."

In fact, Bach's reputation is literally out of this world. In 1977, *Voyager 1* and *2* were launched into deepest space. Each carries a gold-plated record, which will introduce life on this planet to any beings in distant galaxies that might discover it. Part of the record consists of twenty-seven musical selections. Every continent is represented. The choices range from rock 'n roll, jazz, and classical music to a Pygmy girls' initiation song and Australian Aborigine music. But only one composer has three of his works included.

His name is Johann Sebastian Bach. ◆

George Frideric Handel (left) was born the same year as Bach (1685) in Halle, a town less than 60 miles from Bach's birthplace. They have other statistics in common. At the end of their lives, both men lost their eyesight and died after being treated by the same doctor. Both created numerous compositions and both are now regarded as the great exemplars of the Baroque era. Handel, however, led a far different life as a prosperous celebrity. Strangely enough, the two men never met in person.

Martin Luther FYInfo

Martin Luther began the Reformation that eventually resulted in the creation of thousands of Protestant churches in the United States and around the world. Today, the Lutherans form one of the largest Protestant denominations. Johann Sebastian Bach was a devout Lutheran for his entire life. He wrote many of his works to be part of regular church services. "The aim and final end of all music should be none other than the glory of God and the refreshment of the soul," he once wrote.

Luther was born in 1483, two centuries before Bach. He originally planned to become a lawyer and actually started studying law. But he changed his mind and became a priest.

Yet he was soon disappointed with the Catholic Church. He was particularly disturbed by the practice of selling indulgences. For a fee, a person could buy an indulgence and supposedly be guaranteed admittance to heaven. All too often, the money the priests received for indulgences was used to support a lavish lifestyle. Luther believed that this was against the spirit of being a priest. He believed that faith in Jesus Christ was the key to salvation.

In 1517, Luther nailed his famous 95 Theses to the door of the cathedral at Wittenberg, a city in northern Germany. The theses were his specific points of disagreement with what the church was doing. In 1521, he was excommunicated from the church.

Later that year, Luther was forced to appear before a court in the city of Worms, where he was declared an outlaw. He fled for his safety and spent ten months in Wartburg Castle. While he was there, he translated the New Testament of the Bible from its original Greek into German. That way, many more Europeans would be able to read and understand it.

Wartburg Castle is located high on a hill overlooking Eisenach, Bach's birthplace and home for his first ten years. So Johann Sebastian Bach was born almost literally in Martin Luther's shadow. The lives of the two men are connected even though they did not live at the same time.

And there is one direct link between Luther and Bach. In 1529, when he was feeling discouraged, Luther composed the famous hymn "A Mighty Fortress Is Our God." He also wrote a simple musical line to accompany it. Eventually Bach would take Luther's original music and make it much richer. It is now Cantata Number 80 and one of the best-loved hymns in the Lutheran Church.

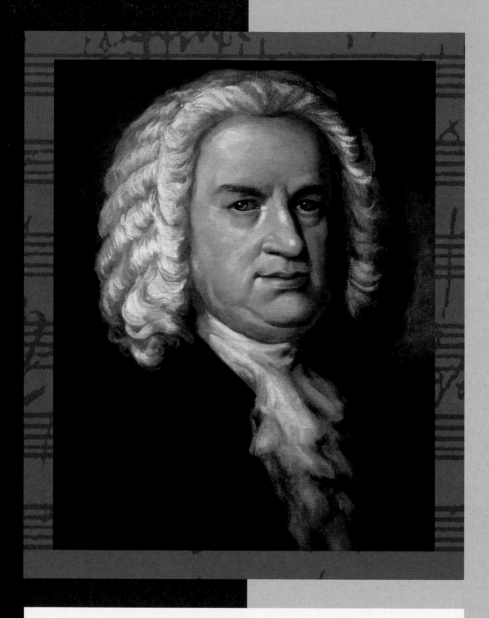

Johann Sebastian Bach came from a large, musical family. Born on March 21, 1685, he was the eighth child born to Johann Ambrosius and Maria Elisabeth. Sadly, his mother died in 1694, when Sebastian was only nine. Though his father remarried, he too died just a year later. Johann Sebastian was orphaned at the age of ten and forced to move in with his older brother, Johann Christoph, from whom he received his first instruction in keyboard-playing.

Masters of Music

CHAPTER 2

A Career in Music Begins

Johann Sebastian Bach was born on March 21, 1685, to Maria Elisabeth and Johann Ambrosius Bach. His father was a church organist and played the violin in the Thuringian town of Eisenach. Thuringia was one of more than 200 small states that would eventually form the modern country of Germany.

The boy was descended from a long line of musicians. The first was Veit Bach, young Sebastian's great-great-grandfather. He was a baker who was born about 1550. He came to Thuringia from Hungary to escape religious persecution. There he learned how to play the zither and the lute.

Soon the family became so numerous and was involved in so many areas of music that the name *Bach* became almost synonymous with the word *musician*. These family connections would later prove valuable to young Sebastian.

Sebastian and his family lived in a large house. A room filled with musical instruments took up much of the first floor. The family slept on the second floor. Not surprisingly, Sebastian learned how to play music at a young age, particularly the violin and keyboard instruments like the organ and harpsichord.

He also began going to the town's Latin School at the age of seven, where he studied reading and writing, Latin grammar, and the Bible. He also sang with the choir at St. George's Church.

Life seemed happy and secure. But that was shattered in 1694.

In that time, sewage and garbage weren't properly disposed of. No one knew of the existence of germs, and it wasn't uncommon for people to die of disease in infancy or early childhood. Johann Sebastian, the youngest of eight children, had already lost two siblings.

Then his mother died suddenly in May 1694. His father— needing help in raising three children who were still at home— quickly remarried. Three months later, in February 1695, Ambrosius Bach died.

Their stepmother, who had children of her own, couldn't keep the family together. Johann Sebastian and his brother Johann Jakob became orphans. They went to live with their older brother, Johann Cristoph, and his wife in the nearby town of Ohrdruf. The brother had a good job as the town's principal organist. He was also an excellent teacher and encouraged his younger brother to keep playing. Sebastian quickly advanced in his ability, easily mastering all the exercises that his brother gave him to practice.

When Sebastian was twelve, his brother bought a book with some complicated new keyboard works by the foremost composers of the day. Because a music book was very expensive, he wouldn't let Sebastian use it for practice. He kept it locked away in a cabinet.

But that didn't stop the youngster. The doors were latticed, formed of thin crisscrossing pieces of wood. Sebastian regularly got up in the middle of the night, reached inside the cabinet, rolled up the book, then pulled it out through the lattice and copied down each composition. It took him six months to finish the task.

His brother caught him and took the manuscript away.

Sebastian also went to school in Ohrdruf, which was considered advanced for its day. He was a good student. He continued to sing in the choir. A few fragments of music show that he was already starting to write his own compositions.

When his brother began having children of his own, there wasn't room for the growing teenager in the small house. Jakob had already moved out and taken a job back in Eisenach. Sebastian may have felt that he had learned all he could in this small town. And he was nearing fifteen, the traditional age at which young men of that era began to support themselves.

The tower of St. George's Church as it appears today. When Johann Sebastian was seven years old, he sang with the church choir at St. George's Church.

Fortunately his choirmaster, Elias Herda, was able to secure a scholarship for him at the St. Michael's School in the town of Lüneburg. Early in 1700, just before his fifteenth birthday, Sebastian and a friend, Georg Erdmann, made the 200-mile journey to the school. They may have been able to hitch an occasional ride with farmers driving ox-drawn wagons, but they probably covered most of the distance on foot.

In Lüneburg, Sebastian joined the St. Michael's Church choir. His voice still hadn't broken, and he had what was regarded as a beautiful soprano voice. As a choir member, he received free school, room and board, and even some spending money when the choir sang at weddings and similar occasions.

Though his voice eventually broke and he had to leave the choir, there was plenty for the fine young musician to do. He played the violin in the local orchestra and accompanied the choir on the harpsichord.

He also had access to the school's music library, where there was no older brother to forbid him from copying music that he could later use to practice. It also gave him some models to study as he began to spend more time as a composer.

He traveled several times to Hamburg, a much larger city with a thriving musical community. He had a cousin who lived there, and he spent many hours listening to a great organist named Johann Adam Reincken.

Because he couldn't afford coach fare, young Sebastian customarily walked the thirty miles each way. According to a story that his children later told, on one of his journeys he stopped outside an inn to rest. He couldn't go inside and eat because he had no money.

Suddenly two herring heads plopped on the ground next to him. He picked them up, hoping to find a few scraps he could gnaw on. What he found was even better. A few coins had been stuffed inside, providing him with enough money to eat and drink and have a little left over. When he looked up to see who had given him this gift, there was no one in sight.

By the time he was almost eighteen, his days as a scholarship boy in the choir were over. It was time to make a living.

He applied for a job as church organist in the town of Sangerhausen in his native Thuringia. As evidence of his ability, he

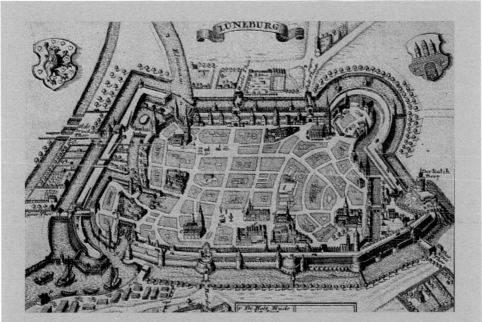

View of Lüneburg about 1650. In the spring of 1700, when Johann Sebastian was 15 years old, he made his way to Lüneburg where he found employment as a choral singer and instrumentalist for church services. Aside from the fine educational facilities here, Lüneburg offered a large library of 1100 musical scores by composers, ancient and contemporary.

was offered the job despite his young age. However, a nobleman objected, insisting that the job be given instead to an older man who was a personal favorite.

In the end, Sebastian accepted an appointment as a court musician with Duke Johann Ernst of Weimar, another Thuringian town. Bach was treated as little more than a servant and he was not permitted to play the organ, but at least it was a paying job.

Four months later, in July 1703, he applied for a position as organist in Arnstadt, about thirty-five miles from Eisenach. Though he was younger than the other applicants, his name worked in his favor. He got the job, signing a contract that paid him more than many experienced musicians.

Along with being an excellent organ player, Bach had a lot of technical expertise in organ design and construction. Pipe organs were among the most complex devices of Bach's day. Extensive renovations had been carried out on organs in Ohrdruf and Lüneburg while he lived there. He helped out with those renovations, acquiring a great deal of useful knowledge. Even as a teenager, he would often be called on to test new organs.

Bach was now a young professional musician. He must have been excited. He had a good job and a lot of free time to compose music.

Another benefit of the job was that many members of his extended family lived in Arnstadt. His stepmother was there. So were relatives descended from his great-uncle Heinrich, the town organist for fifty years until his death when Sebastian was seven.

And there was Maria Barbara Bach, his second cousin.◆

GETTING AROUND

When Johann Sebastian Bach and his friend Georg Erdmann set out to walk the 200 miles from Ohrdruf to Lüneburg in 1700, they probably didn't think they were doing anything unusual. Whenever Bach made the 60-mile round trip from Lüneburg to Hamburg on foot, it must have seemed perfectly natural. Three hundred years ago, muscle power was the most common way to travel. Sometimes people would walk thirty or more miles in a single day.

A few, usually members of the nobility, would use the muscles of other people. They would ride in a sedan chair, a small enclosed compartment with a padded seat, a door and windows. It was mounted on two long poles that stuck out several feet in front and behind. Four men would shoulder the poles and carry the chair.

And of course many people used the muscle power of animals. Many people rode horseback. Others rode in stagecoaches pulled by teams of horses. Farmers and tradesmen used oxen to transport heavy loads.

But even an experienced horseman would rarely cover more than fifty miles a day. For one thing, the roads were terrible. Most were made of dirt. During heavy rains, they became muddy. They often had ruts and potholes. Coach passengers would bounce up and down on their seats. And in winter, they would shiver inside their heavy cloaks because the coaches were not heated.

Besides muscle power, there was one other way of traveling: by water.

Rivers were useful as a means of transportation. It was usually quite easy to load a barge or some other vessel with goods and people and let it drift downstream with the current.

Then there was the sea. By Bach's time, sailing ships were much improved over those that Columbus had used to sail to the New World. But it still took nearly a month to cross the Atlantic Ocean. Traveling by sea could be very dangerous and unpleasant. Severe storms with high winds often sank ships. If there was no wind, the ships would drift helplessly, sometimes for weeks. Ships were commonly infested with rats, cockroaches and other vermin.

It took a lot of effort to travel. It isn't surprising that most people during Bach's lifetime never traveled very far from where they were born.

Of the more than 1000 Bach compositions we know of today, hardly a dozen were published in Bach's lifetime. He had a few of them printed at his own expense. Masterworks like the Well-Tempered Clavier first appeared in print fifty years after his death. His cantatas lay dormant for a century. Many of them were lost due to the carelessness of his heirs. The Bach works that survived were published beginning in 1850 to mark the centennial of the composer's death.

Masters of Music

CHAPTER 3

Growing Fame

In 1705, the Arnstadt town council criticized Johann Sebastian Bach for inviting a "stranger maiden" into the organ loft. We don't know much about Bach's courtship of this young woman. Her identity was never made clear, but some sources indicate that she was Maria Barbara. Others say it was not as she was not "a stranger" in Arnstadt.

This was not the only run-in with authority that Bach had in Arnstadt according to one of his biographers, Philipp Spitta.

In August the previous year, Bach was upset with the way that a young bassoonist named Geyersbach played during a choir rehearsal.

"You sound like a goat," he told him.

Soon afterward, Geyersbach accosted Bach on the street. "I demand an apology," he said.

Bach refused. So Geyersbach said, "You are a cur"—a low form of dog and a definite insult—and bashed him with a stick. Bach pulled a knife, but bystanders separated the two youths before further damage could be done.

Not long after this incident, Bach was given four weeks leave of absence to travel to Lübeck, a north German seaport. It was a journey of well over 200 miles. Bach wanted to hear the famous composer and church organist Dietrich Buxtehude, who was approaching seventy and thinking about retirement. Bach may have wanted to apply for his job.

There was, however, a catch. Whoever replaced Buxtehude as organist would have to marry the old man's daughter, then nearly thirty. In those days, that was very old to be marrying for the first time. Several potential candidates had already passed on the opportunity after seeing her, and Bach was no exception. She was ten years older than he was, and in all likelihood he was in love with Maria Barbara.

Bach stayed well beyond the time that he had been granted, returning more than four months later in February 1706. He had attended many of Buxtehude's concerts and had a number of conversations with the famous man, learning a great deal. He immediately began including some of his new knowledge in his church

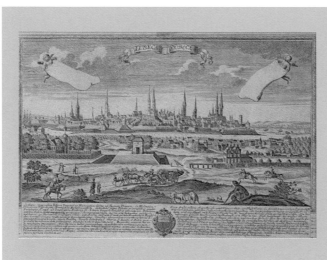

View of Lübeck, where Bach visited in the hopes of meeting the famed organist and composer, Dietrich Buxtehude.

compositions. But his music confused the congregation, which was used to a simpler style.

The council demanded an explanation, both about these "strange sounds" and about his long absence.

Bach offered no apologies. Even as a young man, he already had a stubborn, independent spirit. To his elders on the town council, he must have seemed arrogant. But they didn't want to push him too far.

The final straw may have come later that year. Even though it wasn't in his contract, he was assigned the responsibility for training the boys' choir. It was an unruly bunch. Many of them played ball during church services, casually carried knives into their school classrooms, and drank at taverns. Bach, just a few years older than these young rebels, had little chance at controlling their behavior.

In November 1706, when the council called him to account for the third time for failing to control the boys, Bach probably decided it was time to move on. His compositional skills were rapidly developing, and it was clear that a small town like Arnstadt wouldn't offer him much opportunity to display those skills.

Still, it was during his time at Arnstadt that he composed one of his most famous compositions, the Toccata and Fugue in D Minor. Among other venues, it was selected as the opening sequence for the 1940 Walt Disney film *Fantasia,* which was re-released in 1991.

As fate would have it, the organist at nearby Mühlhausen died the following month. The town council had someone else in mind, but another in the huge chain of Bach relatives served on the council and urged them to give Sebastian an audition. Even though his asking salary was more than what they wanted to pay, he was given the job in the summer of 1707.

A chamber music ensemble during the time that Johann Sebastian Bach was writing many of his compositions. The musicians are gathered around the harpsichord player (second from left). A singer is third from the right. The man in the foreground is playing the viola de gamba, the predecessor of the modern-day cello. Other instruments include (left to right) flute, bassoon, two recorders and a violin.

A month later, one of his great-uncles died and left him an inheritance. Finally he felt secure enough financially to propose to Maria Barbara. They were married that October.

But his job situation wasn't as happy. The pastor at the church where he played believed that music should be very simple. Bach, on the other hand, wanted to compose music that was technically demanding and much more ornate.

Bach auditioned for the orchestra of Duke Wilhelm Ernst of Weimar, the older brother of Duke Johann Ernst, who had employed him four years earlier. He was hired at three times his previous salary.

During his nine months in Mühlhausen, he wrote his first cantata, entitled "God Is My King." Literally, *cantata* means "a piece of music to be sung." In Bach's hands, it would become a combination of dramatic instrumental, choral and solo music. Most of the hundreds of cantatas he wrote were based on religious themes, and the music was carefully matched to the words. Many people consider them closer to opera than to church music.

Soon after arriving at Weimar, the Bachs welcomed their first child, Catharina Dorothea. They would have six more. Tragically, three would die in infancy or early childhood. But all that was in the future.

Bach became the court organist and also played the violin, viola and harpsichord in the orchestra. His relatively light workload left him with plenty of time for composing and other activities, such as teaching and supervising the building and repair of organs and harpsichords.

His reputation as an organist grew. According to one story, a famous Parisian organist named Louis Marchand visited Dresden, one of Germany's largest cities, in 1717. It was more than 100 miles from Weimar.

As his son Carl Philipp Emanuel Bach wrote after his father's death, the visit "gave our Bach, already so famous, a new opportunity to achieve still further honor. . . . The concertmaster in Dresden at the time, Volumier, wrote to Bach and invited him to come forthwith to Dresden, in order to engage in a musical contest for superiority."

Under the terms of the contest, each man would present his rival with music that he hadn't seen before. The members of the court, all of whom were very familiar with the music, would judge which of the two played better.

On the morning of the contest, Bach appeared at the appointed time. Marchand didn't. After an uncomfortable silence, servants were sent to Marchand's quarters to remind him of the contest.

The rooms were empty.

Like a gunfighter in the Old West who lost his nerve at the last moment, Marchand had hired a coach to carry him away from Dresden in the very early hours of the morning. Apparently he couldn't bear the thought of competing against Bach.

It didn't matter.

As C.P.E. Bach concludes, "Bach, who thus remained sole master of the scene of the contest, accordingly had plentiful opportunity to exhibit the talents with which he was armed against his opponent."

Bach and his first three sons. The boy next to him is Johann Gottfried Bernhard. The other two, Carl Philipp Emanuel and Wilhelm Friedemann, became composers. So did Johann Christoph Friedrich and Johann Christian, who were born after this picture was painted.

It was also during this period that Bach composed another great organ work, the Passacaglia and Fugue in C Minor. It is generally regarded as the most demanding organ work ever written. Practically every famous organist today has recorded it at least once.

Despite his fame and growing reputation, Bach was soon forced to move again.

Though the two dukes at Weimar were brothers, they didn't get along at all. Wilhelm Ernst even refused to visit his brother on his deathbed.

Even though the younger duke had been dead for several years, the fraternal feud flared anew in 1717. Bach had remained friendly with Johann Ernst's family. That upset Wilhelm Ernst.

When the duke's kapellmeister, or orchestra leader, died late in 1716, Bach wanted the position. Wilhelm Ernst gave it to the man's son instead. The message was clear: as famous as he was, Bach's possibilities for promotion were nonexistent.

By then, a relative of Johann Ernst had introduced Bach to Prince Leopold of Anhalt-Cöthen. Leopold wanted Bach to become kapellmeister. He offered him a huge salary increase and even began paying him immediately.

But there was a problem: Duke Wilhelm didn't want Bach to go. Bach was insistent, even to the point of impertinence. It was a conflict between two very stubborn men who had one important difference: one of them had all the power. The duke ordered that Bach be arrested in November 1717.

Some accounts say that Bach was kept under house arrest. Others say that the duke had him thrown into jail like a common criminal.

After a month, the duke realized that there was no point in keeping an unhappy musician around. Bach was released and wasted no time in heading for Leopold's court, about fifty miles away.

Prince Leopold was nine years younger than Bach and had also lost his father as a child. His taste in music was well developed, partly the result of having traveled a great deal in his youth. He was an excellent harpsichord and viola da gamba player. He treated his musicians, especially Bach, with high regard.

At the age of thirty-five, Bach's life seemed sweet and serene. He was making excellent money, he had four healthy children, he was composing, and he was court kapellmeister. He was completely in charge of the music at Leopold's court, with one exception: there was no chorus, so he couldn't write sacred music.

In a letter to his old friend Georg Erdmann, Bach wrote a glowing description of those days. "I had a gracious prince, who both loved and knew music, and in his service I intended to spend the rest of my life," he said.

But it was too good to last. ◆

WITCH TRIALS

FYInfo

A notorious series of witch trials took place in 1692 in Salem Village in the colony of Massachusetts. It was one of the darkest periods in early American history.

In January that year, nine-year-old Elizabeth Parris and eleven-year-old Abigail Williams began exhibiting strange symptoms. They would curse, have seizures or go into trances. Soon other girls started acting the same way. Doctors couldn't find anything physically wrong with them. They concluded that the girls were under the influence of Satan.

People in that era believed that Satan could assume the shape of a person and become a witch. Under pressure, the girls pointed to three local women as the culprits. Two denied any wrongdoing. But Tituba, a slave from the West Indies, confessed to being a witch. She also said that other witches were at work in Salem. A wave of hysteria swept through the village. More people were accused of being witches. Within several weeks, more than 100 people had been arrested.

The accused witches were brought before a court that consisted of several prominent citizens. Much of the evidence that was presented was questionable by modern standards. For example, sometimes the girls would throw fits when an accused person appeared in court. No one knew if these fits were genuine or if the girls were just pretending. But there was nothing make-believe about what happened next.

On June 10, Bridget Bishop was hanged as a witch, even though she maintained her innocence. Five more would follow her to the gallows in mid-July. All said they were innocent. And still the court kept on. Five people were hanged in August. In September, eight people were hanged.

Soon afterward, doubts began to surface. The rules of evidence became much tighter. Another trial the following spring didn't convict anyone. The people who had been condemned to death were released.

What happened in Europe was similar. The year 1712 marked the last execution of a witch in England. Two years later, the kingdom of Prussia, not far from Bach's Thuringia, abolished witch trials. Switzerland executed its last witch in 1782.

Though no one is tried for being a witch today, the term *witch hunt* lives on. It usually means using hysteria to go after people with different political beliefs without following normal legal procedures.

This map of Germany shows many of the places that Johann Sebastian Bach lived, worked, or visited during his lifetime. Bach was provincial, a German who never left Germany. When he was young, he traveled on foot to the three northern cities of Lüneburg, Hamburg, and Lübeck. In his later years, he was successful enough to be able to make his journeys in horse-drawn coaches.

Masters of Music

CHAPTER 4

Tragedy and Recovery

I n May 1720, Prince Leopold traveled to the resort town of Carlsbad, a popular vacation site among European aristocrats. Bach accompanied him, leaving his family behind.

When Bach returned to Cöthen in July, horrible news was waiting for him.

Maria Barbara was dead.

The news was shocking. His wife had been in excellent health when he'd left. She had suddenly contracted a serious illness. She had died very quickly and was already buried.

Though he must have been deeply hurt, Bach was a practical man. He couldn't raise his four children by himself. So just over a year later, he married Anna Magdalena Wilcke, a twenty-year-old soprano who sang frequently at the court at Cöthen.

Even though there was a sixteen-year age difference between the two, by all indications theirs was a happy marriage—perhaps even happier than Bach's first. Bach encouraged Anna Magdalena to continue her singing career, and he eventually dedicated two special books of music to her. These are the famous *Anna Magdalena Notebooks*.

In the meantime, Bach finished one of his best-known compositions, the six *Brandenburg Concertos*. They were dedicated to the margrave of Brandenburg, an important nobleman. Perhaps the restless Bach was angling for another job, despite what he would write later about his situation with Leopold.

Leopold himself took a bride one week after Bach and Anna Magdalena were wed. The new princess didn't like music and resented the time that her husband spent with his musicians. She died after just over a year of marriage, but while the friction she'd caused may have abated, Bach had already begun thinking of leav-

Bach is pictured between St. Thomas' Church and the Observatory at Leipzig.
This is an engraving by Albert Henry Payne after a painting by H. Bibby.

A Bach monument, in front of the cantor's office of the St. Thomas School was dedicated in 1837. During the ceremonies, the "last musical Bach," Bach's grandson Wilhelm Friedrich Ernst was honored. He was the only one of Bach's grandsons to achieve musical fame.

ing. His children were growing older and the educational opportunities in Cöthen were limited. In addition, his boys Wilhelm Friedemann and Carl Philipp Emanuel were showing signs of the family musical ability. He wrote a book of keyboard practice pieces for them called *The Well-Tempered Clavier.* It consists of a prelude and fugue for each of the twenty-four key signatures and is still commonly used today.

In June 1722, the cantor of the St. Thomas School and Church in Leipzig died. Bach applied for his job. Despite his fame and reputation, he wasn't the first choice, or even the second. When neither man accepted the job, it was finally offered to him.

These are the main locations where Bach lived and worked in Leipzig. On the left is the St. Thomas School and the St. Thomas Church. Bach lived and worked in the school building along with the choir from 1723 until his death in 1750. The date of this engraving is 1723. In 1730, the building was remodeled and given a new facade. Pictured on the right is the Nikolaikirche, the head church of the town. Bach's first cantata performance as Cantor was given here on May 30, 1723.

At least Bach, who at one time had to walk hundreds of miles because he couldn't afford a coach, got to ride to his new home in style. His arrival in Leipzig in 1723 was written up in the newspapers. Four wagons carried the Bachs' household goods. Two coaches were needed to transport the family. Now, with the recent birth of his first child with Anna Magdalena, there were five children.

When the Bachs moved to Leipzig, it was a town of 30,000 people, one of the largest towns in Germany. Though he didn't realize it, Bach—who had moved five times in the twenty years since leaving Lüneburg—was in the place where he would spend the remaining twenty-seven years of his life.◆

RULE OF THUMB

When Bach was born, there was no reliable method of telling the temperature. Yet during his lifetime, the two most common types of thermometers now in use were invented.

The famous Italian scientist Galileo Galilei actually invented the first "heat measurer" around 1600. It was a tube of water. It was large and cumbersome and not very accurate. In the early 1700s, a Danish scientist named Olaus Rømer made the first practical thermometer. It consisted of wine in a sealed tube. But his scale was unusual. He used 0 degrees for the temperature at which a mixture of ice, salt, and water melted.

Daniel G. Fahrenheit, who was born one year after Bach in 1786, wanted to improve Rømer's work. He divided each of Rømer's degrees into four parts and substituted mercury for the wine. On this new scale, 96 degrees was the average temperature inside the mouth or under the armpit of a healthy person, and 32 degrees was the point at which ordinary ice melted. After he died in 1736, his device was recalibrated, using 212 degrees as the temperature of boiling water as its upper point. That slightly changed the average point of good health to 98.6 degrees. The Fahrenheit scale is still used today in most English-speaking countries.

Most of the rest of the world uses the metric system of measurement. This is where a Swedish astronomer named Anders Celsius, who was born in 1701, comes in. Even though several others had earlier suggested a temperature scale of 0 to 100, Celsius's scientific paper in 1742 firmly established those two points. The unusual thing was that 0 was the boiling point of water and 100 the freezing point. After his death, the scale was turned around, and what became known as the centigrade scale established 0 as the freezing point and 100 as the boiling point. In 1948, it was renamed the Celsius scale in his honor.

It was often unsafe to drink water in Bach's day, and milk could also contain the seeds of illness. As a result, Germans of almost all ages drank beer as naturally as we consume soda today. Yeast is an important element in brewing beer. It has to be added when the mixture is at a certain temperature. Before the invention of the thermometer, brew masters would dip their thumbs into the mixture. On the basis of their experience, they would guess when the temperature was right to add yeast. This is where we get our expression "rule of thumb." The expression is used for a useful gauge that may not be completely accurate.

In May 1747, Bach performed for Frederick II at the royal court. The king asked Bach to improvise a six-part fugue based upon a theme that the king had intoned on his harpsichord. Bach was dissatisfied with his performance and found that the theme was not quite suitable to serve as the basis of a six-part fugue. When Bach returned home to Leipzig, he spent three months composing the Musical Offering which he sent to the Prussian court that fall to make up for his failure on the day of his visit.

Masters of Music

CHAPTER 5

Bach's Legacy

All of Bach's previous moves had been in one direction: up. His earnings had increased each time he had taken a new position. So had his reputation. And at Cöthen, he had enjoyed the freedom to do almost anything musically he wanted to.

That changed at Leipzig. He soon realized that the post paid less than he had anticipated. The family also lost the income that Anna Magdalena's singing had earned at Cöthen. Yet the cost of living was considerably higher than it had been at court or in small towns.

Meanwhile, the demands on his time increased tremendously. He had to organize the boys at the school into choirs for the city's four main churches. He had to furnish music for both church services and civic ceremonies. He had to instruct some of the boys in instrument playing. And he was responsible for teaching them Latin. He didn't want to do that, so he had to pay someone else to take on that part of his job. This was a further drain on the family's finances.

What may have been the biggest blow was that the town council treated him as little more than an employee. He was no longer a kapellmeister, working with a prince who respected his opinions. Instead, he was dealing with a group of small-minded men who had absolutely no idea of his musical genius. Bach was as independent and opinionated as ever, and that led to a number of conflicts during his years in Leipzig.

On the other hand, he was able to return to writing sacred music, which he hadn't been able to do at Cöthen. Most of his great large religious works were composed in Leipzig. These include the Mass in B Minor, the *Christmas Oratorio,* and three dramatic works based on Christ's last seven days on Earth: *St. Mark Passion, St. Luke Passion* and *St. Matthew Passion.* He also wrote most of his sacred cantatas during this period.

This 19th century illustration by Toby E. Rosenthal envisions a Sunday afternoon in the Bach home with Bach at the harpsichord. His grown daughters prepare dinner.

In 1729 Bach became director of the Collegium Musicum. This group of student and professional musicians gave weekly concerts. Most of the concerts were held at one of the new coffeehouses that had sprung up in Leipzig. They were among the first musical performances open to the general public.

In 1730 Bach wrote to his friend Erdmann, who by then was a diplomat living in the seaport city of Danzig (now the Polish city of Gdansk).

"It seemed to me at first not all the right thing to become a Cantor after being a Kapellmeister, but this position was described to me as so favorable that finally I risked myself in the name of the Most High and came to Leipzig," he wrote.

After listing everything that had disappointed him during the succeeding years, he concluded, "If Your Honor should know of or could find a suitable situation in your city for an old and faithful servant, may I humbly request you to put in a gracious recommendation for me?"

Nothing came of the request. It was probably Bach's last effort to get out of Leipzig.

So the years went by. He continued to write music, to perform his duties as cantor, to oversee the building and renovation of organs, and to get into quarrels.

He also continued to have children. Together, he and Anna Magdalena had thirteen. Only six would survive beyond infancy or early childhood. The final child, Regina Susanna, was born in 1742. Having had a total of twenty children between his two wives, he is sometimes referred to as "Papa Bach."

Even though he may not have been appreciated in Leipzig, that wasn't the case elsewhere. His 1747 visit to the court of the Prussian King Frederick II at Potsdam showed the esteem in which the musical world held him.

Soon afterward, the many years of writing and reading music in dim light finally began to take their toll. By the end of 1749 he was virtually blind. The town council of Leipzig began advertising for his replacement.

In desperation, he had two operations on his eyes. They weren't successful. In those days, before the invention of anesthetics, the pain must have been almost unbearable. His health grew even worse, and he died on July 28, 1750.

Bach was buried in an unmarked grave near the church in Leipzig. The location was soon forgotten. Nearly 150 years later, a group of admirers dug up what was believed to be his remains. Several tests confirmed that they were Bach's, and they were reburied in one of Leipzig's churches. The church was destroyed during World War II. Again his remains were rescued and buried in St. Thomas' Church. They are still there today.

Four of his sons—Wilhelm Friedemann, Carl Philipp Emanuel, Johann Christoph Friedrich, and Johann Christian—went on to have successful musical careers. All were also composers, and recordings of their music are sometimes played today.

Johann Christoph Friedrich's son Wilhelm Friedrich Ernst was Bach's only grandchild who continued the family music tradition. Though he lived to the age of eighty-five, he left behind very little music. With his death in 1845, the greatest musical dynasty in history came to an end. It spanned seven generations and nearly 300 years.

Bach's widow, Anna Magdalena, didn't fare very well. Bach left little money behind, and it had to be divided among her and nine surviving children. She died in poverty and obscurity ten years after her husband.

For many years, it appeared that her husband's music would also fall into obscurity. Even his sons regarded their father's music as out of style.

Finally, a young composer named Felix Mendelssohn, then only twenty, conducted a performance of the *St. Matthew Passion* in 1829, almost exactly a century after its premiere. It revived an interest and appreciation for Bach's music that continues today.

Many tributes have come from his fellow composers. Beethoven made a pun on his last name. "Not Bach [German for "brook"] but Meer ["sea"] should be his name," he said.

Johann Christian Bach was Johann Sebastian's youngest son. Christian was just 15 years old when his father died in 1750. Like his father, Christian was taken into the household of an older brother, Carl Philipp Emanuel. Christian totally abandoned his father's heritage. He converted to Catholicism and gained distinction at the English court as a composer of operas and concertos in the Art Galant style.

Twentieth-century composer Paul Hindemith wrote a book about him called *Johann Sebastian Bach: Heritage and Obligation*. In it, he calls Bach a hero, because he constantly had to struggle against obstacles such as those put up by town councils that didn't recognize his genius.

"If music has the power to direct our entire existence toward nobleness, this music is great," Hindemith wrote. "If a composer has dominated his music to this point of greatness, he has achieved the utmost.

"This Bach has achieved."

But perhaps his greatest tribute comes from the thousands and thousands of people who listen to his music every year. They come back to it again and again, marveling at the genius of the German who wrote it.

They assure Johann Sebastian Bach's place among the immortals of music. ◆

Left, St. Thomas' Church as it appears today. On right, statue of Bach by Carl Seffner erected in 1908 that dominates the churchyard. There are numerous statues of Bach in Leipzig today.

FREDERICK
THE GREAT

In 1747, Bach traveled to Potsdam, a city near Berlin. He wanted to visit his son Carl Philipp Emanuel, who was employed as a musician at the court of King Frederick II of Prussia. Eventually Frederick would become known as Frederick the Great.

Frederick considered himself to be a very cultured person. He was interested in writing, philosophy and music. He was not only a music lover but also an excellent flute player and even a composer. He often held evening concerts in which he would play the flute with his orchestra.

He was about to start playing one evening when he learned that Bach had just arrived in the city. He laid down his flute and told the orchestra members, "Gentlemen, old Bach is here." He invited Bach to the palace and let him play each of his seven new pianos. The next day he led a royal procession around Potsdam, inviting Bach to play on all the city's organs.

Bach was pleased with the friendly reception that Frederick had given him. When he returned home he wrote a composition that included parts for the flute so that Frederick could play it. He called it "A Musical Offering."

When Bach was born, what is now Germany consisted of many tiny states and provinces, such as his native Thuringia. One of the largest of these states was Prussia, in the eastern part of Germany. It became a kingdom in 1701, and its first king was Frederick I. He died in 1713 and his son succeeded him, ruling as King Friedrich Wilhelm I.

Just before Freidrich Wilhelm became king, his son Frederick was born, in 1712. Friedrich Wilhelm tried to make a hard soldier of the boy. But through his mother and his governesses, young Frederick learned to speak French and to enjoy literature and music. His father soon began to dislike him intensely and often ridiculed him in public. Things got so bad that when he was eighteen, Frederick tried to escape and go live in England. He was caught and thrown in prison. One of the friends who had tried to help him was beheaded. While Frederick was locked away, his father made him learn the Prussian administrative system. He was released and given command of an army regiment.

As a result, he was well prepared to become king when his father died in 1740. He wasn't as harsh a ruler as his father had been. He eliminated torture, tolerated a wide range of religious beliefs and made the justice system more impartial.

Selected Works

Organ Works
Passacaglia and Fugue in C Minor
Toccata and Fugue in D Minor
Toccata in F

Works for Soloists, Chorus and Orchestra
Christmas Oratorio
St. Matthew Passion
St. John Passion
Mass in B Minor
Magnificat

Cantatas
"Sheep May Safely Graze"
"Jesu Joy of Man's Desiring"
"A Mighty Fortress Is Our God"
"Sleepers Awake"
"Coffee"
"Peasant"

Orchestral Works
Orchestral Suites 1 & 2
Orchestral Suites 3 & 4
Brandenburg Concertos
Concerto for Two Violins
"A Musical Offering"

Keyboard Works
Anna Magdalena Notebook
The Well-Tempered Clavier, Books 1 & 2
Goldberg Variations

Chronology

1685 born on March 21 in Eisenach in German province of Thuringia
1692 enters Eisenach's Latin School
1694 mother dies
1695 father dies; Bach leaves Eisenach to live with brother in Ohrdruf
1700 leaves Ohrdruf for Lüneburg and enrolls in St. Michael's School
1703 is appointed organist in Arnstadt
1705 travels to Lübeck and meets Dietrich Buxtehude
1707 is appointed organist in Mühlhausen; marries Maria Barbara Bach
1708 is appointed organist and chamber musician to Duke Wilhelm Ernst at Weimar; birth of first child, Catharina Dorothea Bach
1714 birth of Carl Philipp Emanuel Bach
1717 is appointed kapellmeister to Prince Leopold at Cöthen
1720 death of wife Maria Barbara
1721 marries Anna Magdalena Wilcke at Cöthen
1723 becomes cantor of St. Thomas' School and Church in Leipzig
1727 his *St. Matthew Passion* premieres at St. Thomas' Church
1729 becomes director of Collegium Musicum
1732 birth of Johann Christoph Friedrich Bach
1742 birth of Regina Susanna Bach, his twentieth and final child
1745 birth of Johann August Bach, his first grandchild
1747 visits court of Frederick the Great at Potsdam
1750 dies on July 28

1517	Martin Luther nails his 95 Theses to a cathedral door at Wittenberg, setting in motion events that become known as the Protestant Reformation
1607	first English settlement in the New World is established at Jamestown, Virginia
1677	ice cream becomes popular as dessert in Paris, France
1685	birth of German composer George Frideric Handel just one month before Bach
1692	Salem witch trials lead to execution of twenty people in Massachusetts Colony
1701	Elector Frederick III of Brandenburg becomes King Frederick I of Prussia
1706	birth of Benjamin Franklin
1707	Scotland and England unite as Great Britain
1709	invention of piano
1712	last execution for witchcraft in England
1719	Daniel Defoe publishes *Robinson Crusoe*
1720	South Sea Bubble, England's first great stock market crash
1726	Jonathan Swift publishes *Gulliver's Travels*
1732	birth of George Washington
1735	birth of Paul Revere and John Adams, who becomes second U.S. president
1740	Frederick II, eventually known as Frederick the Great, becomes King of Prussia
1741	Handel composes *Messiah,* first performed in Dublin in 1742
1743	birth of Thomas Jefferson, who writes Declaration of Independence and becomes third U.S. President
1756	birth of Wolfgang Amadeus Mozart
1765	James Watt invents the steam engine
1770	birth of Ludwig van Beethoven
1776	Declaration of Independence submitted by the thirteen American colonies

Historical Footnote:

The material and financial remains that Bach left behind when he died were not impressive. He left no will so the town sent its official appraisers to his house upon his death. They prepared a *Specification of the Estate* which showed that he left cash of 270 thalers (less than $30,000 today) with an outstanding debt of 150 thalers. It listed his silverware, candlesticks, and cutlery, along with his wardrobe and musical instruments. It did not list his musical works. According to prevailing law, one-third of his estate went to his widow, Anna Magdalena, who was 49 years old. The rest was divided equally among his children. In the library at St. Thomas' Church, Bach had assembled the vocal scores of many of his cantatas, filed in impeccable order, each clearly marked. Bach's successor must have decided that this "old stuff" was taking up too much shelf space and he disposed of numerous manuscripts. Some manuscripts were even reported to have made their way to a butcher shop and used for wrapping paper. Because of this bungling, Anna Magdalena's declining years were sad ones and when she died, she was buried in an unmarked pauper's grave.

For Further Reading

For Young Adults:

Catucci, Stefano. *Bach and Baroque Music*. New York: Barrons Juvenile, 1998.

Patton, Barbara. *Introducing . . . Johann Sebastian Bach*. Sunnyvale, Calif.: Soundboard Books, 1992.

Reingold, Carmel Berman. *Johann Sebastian Bach: Revolutionary of Music*. New York: Franklin Watts, 1970.

Vernon, Roland. *Introducing Bach*. Parsippany, N.J.: Silver Burdett Press, 1996.

Works Consulted:

The stories about Johann Sebastian Bach related in this book have been passed down through many references on the composer's life. There are literally hundreds of biographies written about Bach. By the early years of the twentieth century, two monumental biographies had been published. The first was written by pioneer music historian Philipp Spitta and the second by the great organist and humanitarian Albert Schweitzer. Both of these works continue to be regarded as classics and many of the newer works have relied on the information presented in these two stalwarts. The author has retold versions of Bach's life found in the following sources.

Bettmann, Otto L. *Johann Sebastian Bach as His World Knew Him*. New York: Carol Publishing Group, 1995.

Blom, Eric (ed.). *Grove's Dictionary of Music and Musicians*. New York: St. Martin's Press, 1954.

Hindemith, Paul. *Johann Sebastian Bach: Heritage and Obligation*. London: Oxford University Press; New Haven: Yale University Press, 1952.

Headington, Christopher. *J. S. Bach*. New York: Pavilion Books, 1994.

Wolff, Christoph. *Johann Sebastian Bach: The Learned Musician*. New York: W. W. Norton & Company, 2000.

Internet Sites:

Bach's Travels: http://odur.let.rug.nl/Linguistics/diversen/bach/map.html

Bach's education and career: http://jan.ucc.nau.edu/~tas3/life.html

Brief biography and links: http://www.classical.net/music/comp.lst/bachjs.html

Summary of Bach's life: http://www.baroquemusic.org/bqxjsbach.html

Biography, portraits, timeline: http://www.jsbach.org/

For Researchers:

Schweitzer, Albert. *J.S. Bach*, trans. Ernest Newman, New York: Macmillan, (first published in German 1873-1880) 1950.

Spitta, Philipp. *Johann Sebastian Bach: His Work and Influence on the Music of Germany*. New York: Dover Books, (first published in 1905) 1951.

Glossary

audition (aw-DISH-in)—a tryout for a musical position.

behemoth (beh-HEE-muth)—something very large.

cantata (kan-TAH-tah)—a choral work composed of both solo and chorus parts.

cantor (KAN-ter)—a director of music at a German Protestant church.

clavichord (KLAH-vih-kord)—the earliest keyboard instrument that uses strings to produce sounds.

clavier (kleh-VIR)—a keyboard instrument, usually referring to the clavichord or harpsichord.

excommunicated (ex-kom-MUNE-i-kate-ed)—to be cut off from a group, especially a church, as a punishment for one's beliefs or actions.

fugue (FYOOG)—a piece of music that begins with a single tune. As it develops, another musical line playing the same tune joins in. Eventually it can have three or four lines, all based on the original tune.

harpsichord (HARP-si-kord)—a keyboard instrument like a piano on which the strings are plucked instead of struck.

improvise (IM-proe-vize)—to make up something on the spot without any preparation.

kapellmeister (keh-PELL-my-ster)—the leader of an orchestra at the court of a nobleman.

key signature (kee SIG-nuh-chur)—a particular grouping musical tones; for most modern-day music, there are twenty-four key signatures in all, identified by a capital letter from A through G and other notations, which may include *sharp, flat, major,* or *minor.*

lute (LOOT)—a pear-shaped stringed musical instrument.

oratorio (or-ah-TOR-ee-oh)—a complex, large-scale musical composition for orchestra, chorus and soloists, usually based on a religious theme.

passacaglia (pah-seh-KAHL-ye)—a musical form consisting of continuous variations of an original tune.

prelude (PRAY-lewd)—a piece of music intended to introduce another piece.

soprano (seh-PRAH-noh)—the highest singing voice among the five levels of singers; the others in descending order are alto, tenor, baritone and bass.

toccata (tah-KAH-tah)—musical form derived from Italian word *toccare,* which means "to touch"; usually used to demonstrate keyboard touch technique.

viola de gamba (vee-OH-leh deh-GAHM-beh)—a stringed instrument held between the knees, similar to the modern cello.

zither (ZIH-ther)—a musical instrument with up to forty strings stretched over a flat soundboard similar to that of a guitar but played in a horizontal position.

Index